MW01044830

30018000321 58V

WITHDRAWN

SHOCKWAVE
SOCIAL STUDIES

Made by Humans

Astonishing Achievements

© 2008 Weldon Owen Education Inc. All rights reserved.

No part of this publication may be reproduced or transmitted
in any form or by any means, electronic or mechanical,
including photocopying, recording, taping, or any information storage
and retrieval system, without permission in writing from the publisher.

Library of Congress Cataloging-in-Publication Data

Allison, Carol J.
  Made by humans : astonishing achievements / by Carol J. Allison.
        p. cm. -- (Shockwave)
  Includes index.
  ISBN-10: 0-531-17789-0 (lib. bdg.)
  ISBN-13: 978-0-531-17789-1 (lib. bdg.)
  ISBN-10: 0-531-15477-7 (pbk.)
  ISBN-13: 978-0-531-15477-9 (pbk.)

  1. Engineering--Juvenile literature. 2. Architecture--Juvenile
literature. I. Title. II. Series.

  TA149.A45 2007
  624--dc22

2007012227

Published in 2008 by Children's Press, an imprint of Scholastic Inc.,
557 Broadway, New York, New York 10012
www.scholastic.com

SCHOLASTIC, CHILDREN'S PRESS, and associated logos are trademarks
and/or registered trademarks of Scholastic Inc.

08 09 10 11 12 13 14 15 16 17
10 9 8 7 6 5 4 3 2 1

Printed in China through Colorcraft Ltd., Hong Kong

Author: Carol J. Allison
Educational Consultant: Ian Morrison
Editor: Nerida Frost
Illustrators: Xiangyi Mo and Jingwen Wang
Designer: Miguel Carvajal
Photo Researchers: Jamshed Mistry and Sarah Matthewson

Photographs by: Aapimage.com: AFP PHOTO/HO/Samsung Corp (p. 31); **Anne Luo**
(p. 11); **BLS AlpTransit AG, Thun** (p. 29); **Corel** (p. 13); **Getty Images** (pyramid,
pp. 16–17); **Jennifer and Brian Lupton** (teenagers, pp. 32–33); **Photodisc** (p. 7);
Photolibrary (New York skyline, pp. 24–25); **Stock.Xchng.com** (p. 5, p. 34); **Tranz/Corbis**
(cover; p. 3; pp. 8–11; pp. 14–15; skeletons, p. 17; pp. 18–20; pp. 22–23; construction
worker, p. 25; pp. 26–28; p. 30; shrine, p. 32–33)

The publisher would like to thank BLS AlpTransit AG, Thun for the use of the photograph
of Lötschberg Tunnel workers on page 29.

All illustrations and other photographs © Weldon Owen Education Inc.

SHOCKWAVE
SOCIAL STUDIES

Made by Humans

Astonishing Achievements

Carol J. Allison

Gordon Gregory Middle School
26 Farmingdale Circle
Naperville, IL 60564

WITHDRAWN

children's press®

An imprint of Scholastic Inc.

NEW YORK • TORONTO • LONDON • AUCKLAND • SYDNEY
MEXICO CITY • NEW DELHI • HONG KONG
DANBURY, CONNECTICUT

CHECK THESE OUT!

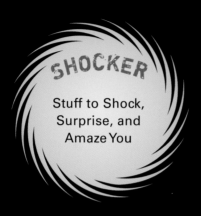

SHOCKER
Stuff to Shock,
Surprise, and
Amaze You

Quick Recaps
and Notable
Notes

Word Stunners
and Other Oddities

?

The Heads-Up
on Expert Reading

Links to More
Information

CONTENTS

archaeologist (*ar kee OL uh jist*) a scientist who studies people and objects from the past

culture (*KUHL chur*) the way of life, ideas, and customs of a people

fortress a place that is strengthened against attack

prehistoric belonging to a time before history was written down

pyramid (*PIHR uh mid*) a massive monument with a square base and four triangular walls, with inner burial chambers

restore to bring back to an original condition

For additional vocabulary, see Glossary on page 34.

The *pre-* in *prehistoric* means "before." Some words use the prefix *post-*, meaning "after." More examples of words with these prefixes are: *prepay, prewar, postwar, postscript.*

The **fortress** of El Morro, Santiago de Cuba, Cuba

People have been building astonishing structures since ancient times. These wonders all over the world help us to understand what was important to the people of the past. Temples and tombs give us information about past ways of life.

In modern times, people also wish to build great works of architecture. New technology has helped to change landscapes. Projects still under way are leading us into the future. Some of these will change our world in many exciting ways.

The temple of Angkor Wat, Cambodia

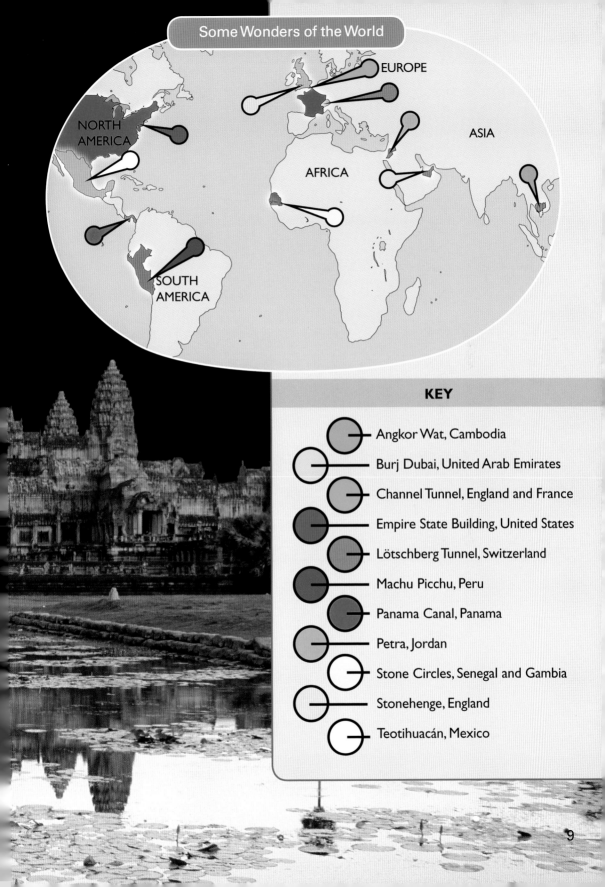

EUROPE

NORTH
AMERICA

ASIA

AFRICA

SOUTH
AMERICA

KEY

- Angkor Wat, Cambodia
- Burj Dubai, United Arab Emirates
- Channel Tunnel, England and France
- Empire State Building, United States
- Lötschberg Tunnel, Switzerland
- Machu Picchu, Peru
- Panama Canal, Panama
- Petra, Jordan
- Stone Circles, Senegal and Gambia
- Stonehenge, England
- Teotihuacán, Mexico

9

Ring of Stones

Stonehenge, England: 2800–1500 B.C.

How did huge stone blocks come to stand in a ring on a plain in England? Who brought them there, and why? This ancient monument is Stonehenge. It is a true wonder of **prehistoric** construction. **Archaeologists** have figured out what Stonehenge looked like originally.

Stonehenge is in ruins today. Only half the stones are left, but it is still a marvel to many who see it. The British government started protecting Stonehenge in 1922.

Wales

England

Stonehenge

The outside circle was made up of large stones. Laid flat across the tops of these **monoliths** were other stones, called lintels. Inside this circle was another, called the bluestone circle. It was made up of as many as 84 smaller stones. Inside the bluestone circle was a horseshoe of giant stones and lintels. Finally, there was a smaller horseshoe of bluestones.

Did You Know?

There are also prehistoric stone circles in Africa. More than 1,000 stones are spread over a huge area along the Gambia River in Senegal and Gambia. The stone circles date from 300 B.C. to 1500 A.D. They are on the UNESCO World Heritage List.

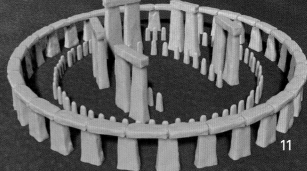

This is how archaeologists think Stonehenge looked originally.

How was Stonehenge built? The bluestones weigh about four tons each. This is as much as four schoolbuses! They came from a place in Wales, more than 240 miles away. The giant stones weigh up to 40 tons. They probably came from about 25 miles away. Experts think that the bluestones were brought from Wales by water. Apparently, the giant stones were moved using only levers, sleds, and rollers.

Experts believe:

- the bluestones came from Wales
- the bluestones were brought by water

Experts know:

- the bluestones weighed about 4 tons
- the giant stones weighed about 40 tons

For hundreds of years, people have wondered what the purpose of Stonehenge was. Was it used for religious **ceremony** or for **astronomy**? No **theories** have been proven. Why it was built remains a mystery to this day.

SHOCKER

In the year 2000, an attempt to recreate the 240-mile journey of a bluestone failed. The bluestone fell into the sea! One newspaper headline read:
*Ancient Britons – 84 stones
Modern Britons – 0 stones*

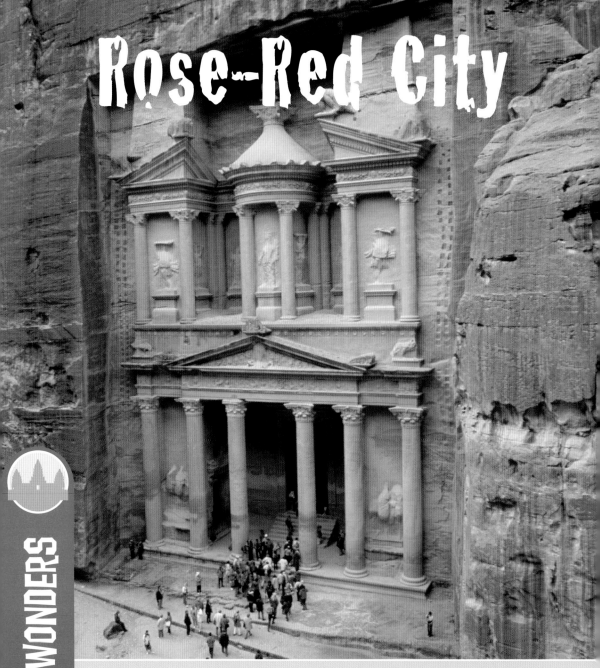

Rose-Red City

Petra, Jordan: 400 B.C.

It sounds like an adventure movie, but it was real life.
In 1812, a young Swiss man was traveling in Jordan.
Johann Ludwig Burckhardt heard talk of a mysterious, lost city.
He set out to find it. When his guides led him out of a long,
steep **gorge**, he saw an astonishing sight.

An entire city of temples, tombs, and caves was carved into the cliffs. The local people had kept this wonder a secret for more than 600 years. The name of the city was Petra, which means "rock" in Greek.

Petra had been a successful trading center from about 400 B.C. to 200 A.D. By 700 A.D., it had lost its importance. By 1200 A.D., it had been deserted. When Burckhardt came upon Petra, it was partly buried under sand and rocks. An early visitor called Petra the "rose-red city." This was because the sandstone looked so red in the sun.

Syria

Israel

Jordan

Petra

Saudi Arabia

The word *petrified* also comes from the Greek language. It means "turned to stone." It also refers to someone who is really, really scared.

Painting of Petra, 1839

City of the Gods

Teotihuacán (*Tay oh tee wah KAHN*), Mexico: 500 A.D.

Imagine a city with **pyramids,** palaces, and apartment buildings. It covers an area of eight square miles. Its streets are laid out in a grid. No, this is not a modern, high-tech city. It is a city that thrived in Mexico 1,500 years ago. It is known as Teotihuacán.

Oh, yeah! I remember what a square mile is. It doesn't mean that the city is in the shape of a square. Eight square miles could be four miles long and two miles wide. I didn't think math would help with reading.

United States

Mexico

Teotihuacán

Mexico City

N

In its day, Teotihuacán was the most powerful city in the Americas. It was a wealthy and important religious center. However, by about 800 A.D., the city was deserted.

In the 1400s and 1500s, the Aztecs ruled a great empire in Mexico. When they arrived in Teotihuacán, its pyramids and palaces lay in ruins. However, the Aztecs could see that it had once been a great and sacred place. So they named it Teotihuacán, "City of the Gods."

SHOCKER

In 2004, archaeologists made a horrifying discovery at Teotihuacán. They found the remains of human **sacrifices**. All the bodies had their hands tied behind their backs.

Jungle Temple

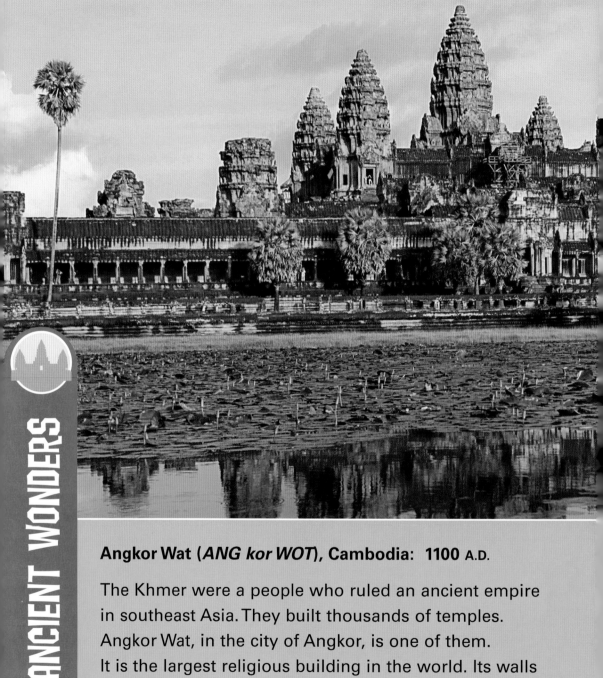

Angkor Wat (*ANG kor WOT*), Cambodia: 1100 A.D.

The Khmer were a people who ruled an ancient empire in southeast Asia. They built thousands of temples. Angkor Wat, in the city of Angkor, is one of them. It is the largest religious building in the world. Its walls are nearly half a mile long. Angkor Wat was built to honor **Hindu** gods. Later, it became a **Buddhist** temple.

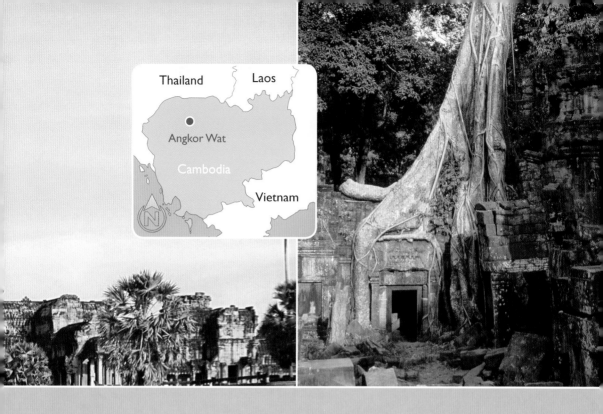

The city of Angkor was deserted in the 1400s. However, **pilgrims** continued to visit the temple itself. The outside world knew little about Angkor until the late 1800s. Then French **naturalist** Henri Mouhot wrote about it in his travel journals. They sparked the interest of the world. When Angkor was rediscovered, it was so overgrown that trees were growing on the buildings. Archaeologists started to **restore** it. Today, Angkor Wat is a place of prayer. It is also a UNESCO World Heritage Site.

Angkor Wat is very important to the Cambodian people.

Supporting statements:
• pilgrims continued to visit
• city was restored
• UNESCO World Heritage Site

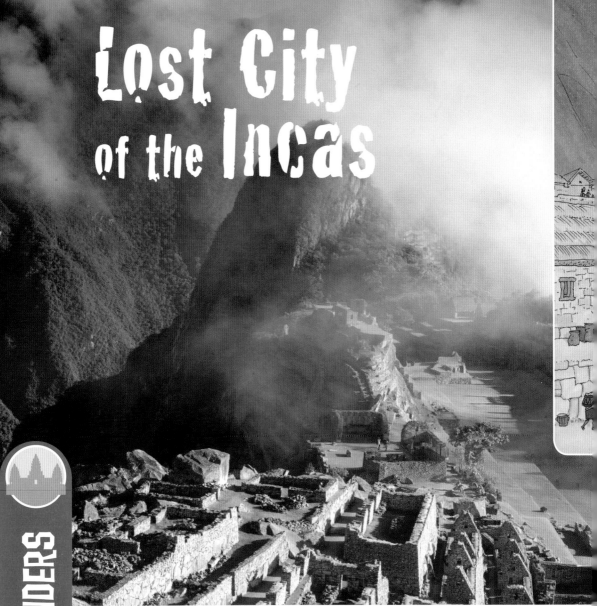

Lost City of the Incas

Machu Picchu (*Ma choo PEEK choo*), Peru: 1450–1540 A.D.

Machu Picchu was a **fortress** city in the Andes Mountains of Peru. It was built by an ancient people called the Incas. The Incas ruled a vast empire in South America in the 1400s and 1500s. Machu Picchu was probably a **refuge** for Inca royalty. There were more than 140 buildings, where at least 700 people lived. Its location in the mountains made it safe from attack.

SHOCKER

Spanish explorers took potatoes back to Europe from South America. At first, Europeans were afraid to eat them. They thought that they were poisonous. In fact, the part that we eat is the only part of the potato plant that is *not* poisonous!

The Incas built terraces on the mountains to grow crops.

Ecuador
Colombia
Peru
Brazil
Machu Picchu
Bolivia

The Incas were master builders. They were also experts at growing crops, such as potatoes, on the mountains. No one knows why Machu Picchu was abandoned around 1540. The outside world forgot about the city for nearly 400 years. It was rediscovered in 1911 by an American archaeologist, Hiram Bingham II.

World's Greatest
Shortcut

I thought shortcuts were just something kids were interested in, like a shortcut across the playing field. I already know that shortcuts save time and effort. Knowing this will make these pages easier to understand.

Panama Canal, Panama: 1914

For centuries, the sea journey from the Atlantic Ocean to the Pacific Ocean was very long and dangerous. Ships had to go all the way around the southern tip of South America. As early as the 1500s, people dreamed of building a canal through Central America to connect the two oceans.

MODERN WONDERS

The Panama Canal cuts through the **Isthmus** of Panama. There are three sets of locks in the canal. They raise and lower ships to the different levels of water through the canal.

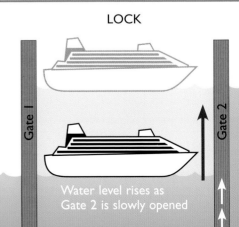

LOCK

Gate 1

Gate 2

Sea level

Water level rises as Gate 2 is slowly opened

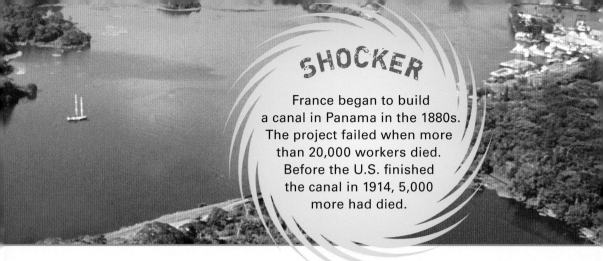

SHOCKER

France began to build a canal in Panama in the 1880s. The project failed when more than 20,000 workers died. Before the U.S. finished the canal in 1914, 5,000 more had died.

It took hundreds of years to make the dream come true. People could not agree on where to build the canal, or who should control it. Projects started and failed. Digging machines were too small. Thousands of workers died of diseases. Companies ran out of money.

In 1903, the United States helped Panama get its independence from Colombia. In return, Panama gave the United States control of a canal zone. In 1906, the United States started building the canal. Better machines and medical knowledge about disease helped the project to succeed. In 1914, the 50-mile canal was finished. The Panama Canal took 8,000 miles off the trip from New York to San Francisco. Now that's a shortcut!

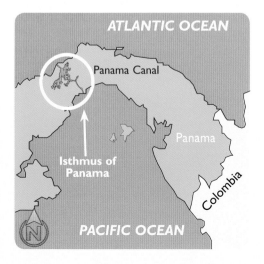

23

Skyscraper
Supreme

The Empire State Building, U.S.A.: 1931

It has become one of the most well-known buildings in the world. It has appeared in more than 75 movies. When it was built, people couldn't believe how high it was. The Empire State Building changed the skyline of New York. It became a symbol of the modern age.

The Empire State Building was designed in the Art Deco style. This style was ultramodern for the time. Art Deco was the sleek new look of the 1930s.

In the late 1800s, two new inventions made it possible for people to build skyscrapers. These inventions were steel frames and elevators. With these two things, the race was on to build the world's tallest building!

Two businessmen in the United States, John Raskob and Walter Chrysler, joined the race. When the Empire State Building was finished in 1931, Raskob had won it. The Empire State Building was 1,250 feet high. It was 204 feet higher than Walter Chrysler's building. The Empire State Building was the tallest building in the world for 41 years.

SHOCKER

Workers on the Empire State Building didn't have safety equipment. Surprisingly, only five people died during construction. Today, workers on skyscrapers never work without safety lines.

Canada

Empire State Building

New York City

United States

The Chunnel

Channel Tunnel, France and England: 1994

The high-speed train races through the tunnel at 100 miles per hour. You can feel your ears pop. You have just left France. In only 20 minutes, you will be in England.
You are traveling through the Channel Tunnel. At 31 miles long, it is the world's longest undersea rail tunnel.
The Chunnel is made up of three tunnels. There are two train tunnels and a service-and-emergency tunnel.

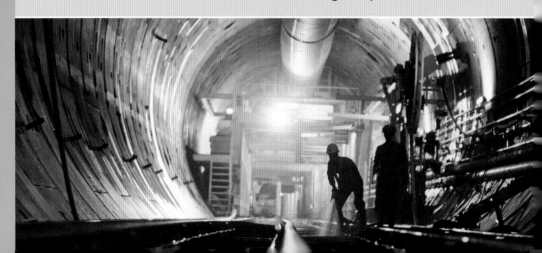

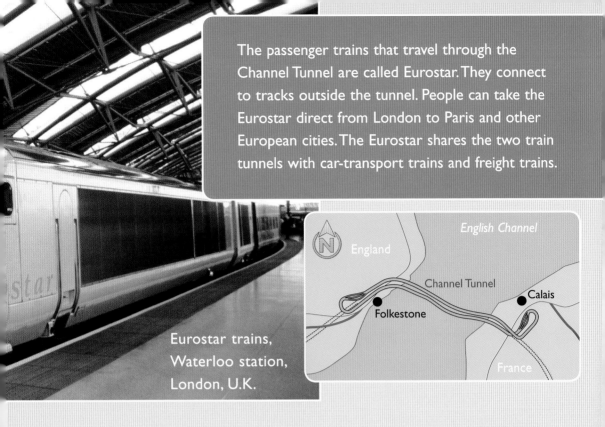

The passenger trains that travel through the Channel Tunnel are called Eurostar. They connect to tracks outside the tunnel. People can take the Eurostar direct from London to Paris and other European cities. The Eurostar shares the two train tunnels with car-transport trains and freight trains.

Eurostar trains, Waterloo station, London, U.K.

The idea of a tunnel between France and England is not new. It was first suggested in the 1700s! For more than 200 years, people tried to come up with a plan for linking the two countries. Digging started twice. It was stopped because of money, politics, or technical problems. Finally, in 1987, work began on the Chunnel, as it is called. It took nearly seven years to complete. The Channel Tunnel was opened with a big celebration in 1994.

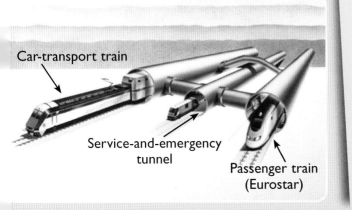

Car-transport train

Service-and-emergency tunnel

Passenger train (Eurostar)

I now know that the Channel Tunnel:

- is the world's longest undersea rail tunnel
- connects France and England
- opened in 1994
- has trains traveling through it at more than 100 mph

Lötschberg Tunnel, Switzerland: 2007

In April 2005, an explosion blew through 12 feet of granite.
A huge cheer went up. It had taken 11 years, drilling from
opposite ends. Workers had bored 21 miles through
the Swiss Alps. The Lötschberg Tunnel opened in 2007.
It is the longest land tunnel in the world.

Route of the Lötschberg Tunnel, through the Swiss Alps

North Entrance

Frutigen

Lötschber;

21 miles

Switzerland is in the center of Europe. Traffic through the country is very heavy. The Swiss have come up with a plan to save the Alps from traffic and pollution. They are moving trucks off the roads and onto the railroads.

In the Lötschberg Tunnel, trucks will be loaded onto trains at one end. They will be unloaded at the other. This is much safer than having many big trucks on the roads. It will also make the trip from Germany to Italy much shorter. The Lötschberg Tunnel will help to keep the beautiful Swiss Alps safe and clean.

I hope the workers weren't *bored* as they *bored* through the rock. Many words, such as *bore*, have several meanings.

France

Germany

Switzerland

Frutigen

Lötschberg Tunnel

Raron

Italy

N

South Entrance

Raron

ALTITUDE

8,200 feet

1,968 feet

0 feet

Burj Dubai, United Arab Emirates: 2009

Burj is the Arabic word for "tower." When it is finished, the Burj Dubai will be the world's tallest structure. No one knows for sure how tall it will be. The builders are keeping it a secret!

Some say that it will be almost half a mile high! However, the builders will change the plans to make it taller if need be. The **foundations** are extra deep to allow for this. Burj Dubai isn't finished yet, so there are only artists' impressions of what it will look like.

FUTURE WONDER

Dubai

Qatar

Persian Gulf

Burj Dubai

United Arab Emirates

Saudi Arabia

Oman

Famous Skyscrapers of the World

Height (feet)

2,500
2,000
1,500
1,000
500
Ground level

Burj Dubai

CN Tower
Canada

Taipei 101
Taiwan

Empire State
Building, U.S.A.

The tower will be spiral-shaped to prevent strong winds
from building up around it. Like most new buildings in Dubai,
it will be ultraluxurious. It will have an observation deck
on the 124th floor. There will be double-decker elevators, as well
as the world's fastest elevator. Burj Dubai will have immense
cooling systems. Dubai is very hot, so cold water is a luxury!

People today want to create **impressive** monuments, just as ancient people did. Modern technology helps them to achieve their goals. Structures are getting bigger, taller, and longer. However, huge structures change the landscape in a huge way. We lose green spaces and the wildlife that goes with them.

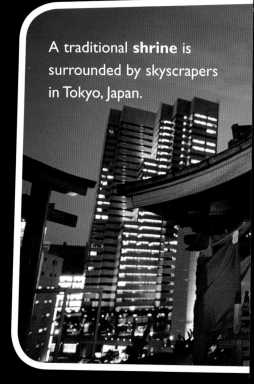

A traditional **shrine** is surrounded by skyscrapers in Tokyo, Japan.

WHAT DO YOU THINK?

Is bigger always better, when it comes to building the cities of the future?

PRO

As technology improves, we should use it to create modern wonders of architecture. These projects can help improve living conditions for many people. Big international projects will also lead to better understanding between people of different countries.

All over the world, large parts of old cities are being torn down to make way for mega-structures. Buildings from the past are disappearing. Organizations such as UNESCO are working hard to save many of them. Yet cities in different parts of the world are starting to look more and more similar.

CON

Buildings should fit into the landscape. They should suit the local **culture**. Building projects should change nature as little as possible. We should be using modern technology to restore and protect the environment.

33

GLOSSARY

astronomy the study of stars, planets, and space

Buddhist (*BOO dist*) to do with Buddhism, a religion that follows the teachings of the Indian teacher Buddha

ceremony formal actions, words, and often music, performed to mark an important occasion

foundation a solid structure on which a building is built

gorge (*GORJ*) a deep valley with steep, rocky sides

Hindu (*HIN doo*) to do with Hinduism, a religion practiced mainly in India

impressive attracting attention or admiration

isthmus (*ISS muhss*) a narrow strip of land between two bodies of water that connects two larger land masses

monolith (*MON uh lith*) a single massive block of stone

naturalist someone who studies animals and plants

pilgrim a person who goes on a journey to worship at a holy place

refuge (*REF yooj*) a place that provides protection or shelter from danger or trouble

sacrifice an offering of something to God or a god

shrine a holy building that often contains sacred objects

theory an idea based on some facts, but not proved

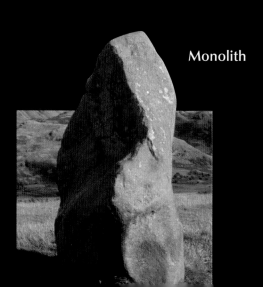

Monolith

FIND OUT MORE

BOOKS

Allison, Carol J. *Mighty Earth*. Scholastic Inc., 2008.

Ash, Russell. *Great Wonders of the World*. Dorling Kindersley, 2006.

Curlee, Lynn. *Skyscraper*. Atheneum Books for Young Readers, 2007.

Llewellyn, Claire. *Great Discoveries and Amazing Adventures*. Kingfisher, 2004.

Mann, Elizabeth. *The Panama Canal*. Mikaya Press, 2006.

Petrini, Catherine M. *Stonehenge*. KidHaven Press, 2005.

Silate, Jennifer. *Inca Ruins of Machu Picchu*. KidHaven Press, 2005.

WEB SITES

 Go to the Web sites below to learn more about wonders of the world.

www.esbnyc.com/kids

www.pancanal.com/eng/persona/k

www.oneworldheritage.com

http://library.thinkquest.org/5983

INDEX

ABOUT THE AUTHOR

Carol J. Allison has lived in many areas of the United States and has traveled to several other countries. As an author of fiction and nonfiction books for children, Carol also "travels the world" through Internet resources and library research in her quest for learning more about the fascinating places in our world. She encourages students to use their own resources to learn more about how and why humans built these awesome structures, and what the structures tell us about civilizations past and present.